World Series Champions: St. Louis Cardinals

Pitcher Bob Gibson

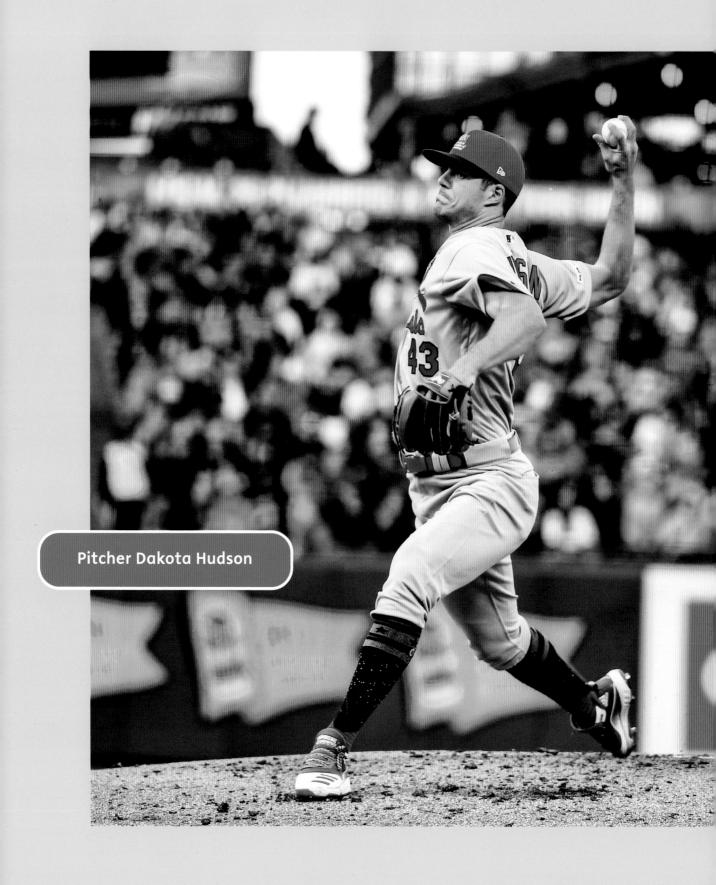

Pitcher Dakota Hudson

WORLD SERIES CHAMPIONS

ST. LOUIS CARDINALS

MICHAEL E. GOODMAN

CREATIVE EDUCATION / CREATIVE PAPERBACKS

Published by Creative Education and Creative Paperbacks
P.O. Box 227, Mankato, Minnesota 56002
Creative Education and Creative Paperbacks are imprints of
The Creative Company
www.thecreativecompany.us

Art Direction by Tom Morgan
Book production by Ciara Beitlich
Edited by Joe Tischler

Photographs by Alamy (Cal Sport Media, UPI), Corbis (Diamond
Images, Robert Riger), Dreamstime (f11photo), Getty (Bettmann,
Elsa, G Fiume, Focus on Sport, Otto Greule Jr., Thearon W.
Henderson, National Baseball Hall of Fame, Ezra Shaw)

Library of Congress Cataloging-in-Publication Data
Names: Goodman, Michael E., author.
Title: St. Louis Cardinals / Michael E. Goodman.
Description: Mankato, MN : Creative Education and Creative
    Paperbacks, [2024] | Series: Creative sports. World Series
    champions | Includes index. | Audience: Ages 7-10 | Audience:
    Grades 2-3 | Summary: "Elementary-level text and engaging sports
    photos highlight the St. Louis Cardinals' MLB World Series wins and
    losses, plus sensational players associated with the professional
    baseball team such as Albert Pujols." -- Provided by publisher.
Identifiers: LCCN 2023011813 (print) | LCCN 2023011814 (ebook) | ISBN
    9781640268357 (library binding) | ISBN 9781682773857 (paperback)
    | ISBN 9781640269880 (pdf)
Subjects: LCSH: St. Louis Cardinals (Baseball team)--History--Juvenile
    literature. | World Series (Baseball)--History--Juvenile literature.
Classification: LCC GV875.S74 G663 2024 (print) | LCC GV875.S74
    (ebook) | DDC 796.357/640977866--dc23/eng/20230313
LC record available at https://lccn.loc.gov/2023011813
LC ebook record available at https://lccn.loc.gov/2023011814

Printed in China

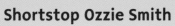

CONTENTS

Home of the Cardinals

St. Louis, Missouri, is a large city in the Midwest. A beautiful 600-foot **arch** rises above the city. Busch **Stadium** is located near there. It is home to a baseball team called the Cardinals.

The St. Louis Cardinals are a Major League Baseball (MLB) team. They compete in the National League (NL) Central Division. Their **rivals** are the Chicago Cubs. All MLB teams want to win the World Series and become champions. The Cardinals have won the World Series 11 times!

Outfielder/First baseman Stan Musial

Naming the Cardinals

he team first played in 1882. Players wore brown socks and hats. Then, new owners made a change. They had players dress in bright red socks and shirts with red trim. One writer said they looked like lively red birds called cardinals. Soon everyone started calling the team the "Cardinals," or "Cards," for short.

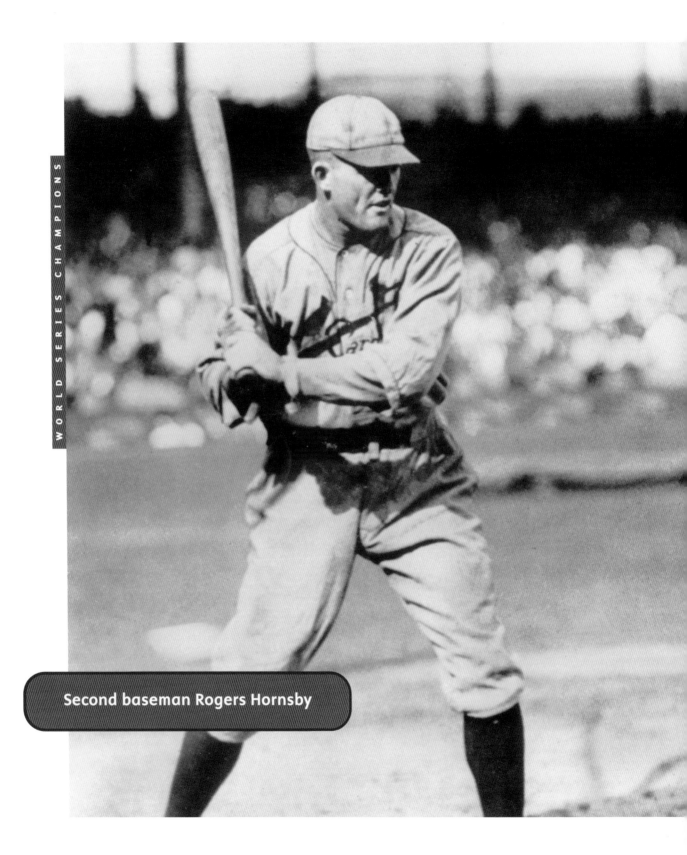

Second baseman Rogers Hornsby

Cardinals History

The club was first known as the Brown Stockings. In 1900, they became the Cardinals. They had many losing seasons. Then, in 1915, hard-hitting second baseman Rogers Hornsby joined the team. He led the NL in batting six times for St. Louis. He even batted over .400 three times! In 1926, Hornsby played for and managed the team. He pushed them to their first World Series **title**.

The Cardinals captured two more championships in the 1930s. Dizzy Dean led the way in 1934. He is the last NL pitcher to win 30 games in a season. The Cards earned three more titles in the 1940s. They were led by outfielder Stan "the Man" Musial. He played 22 seasons in St. Louis. He was chosen as an All-Star 20 of those years.

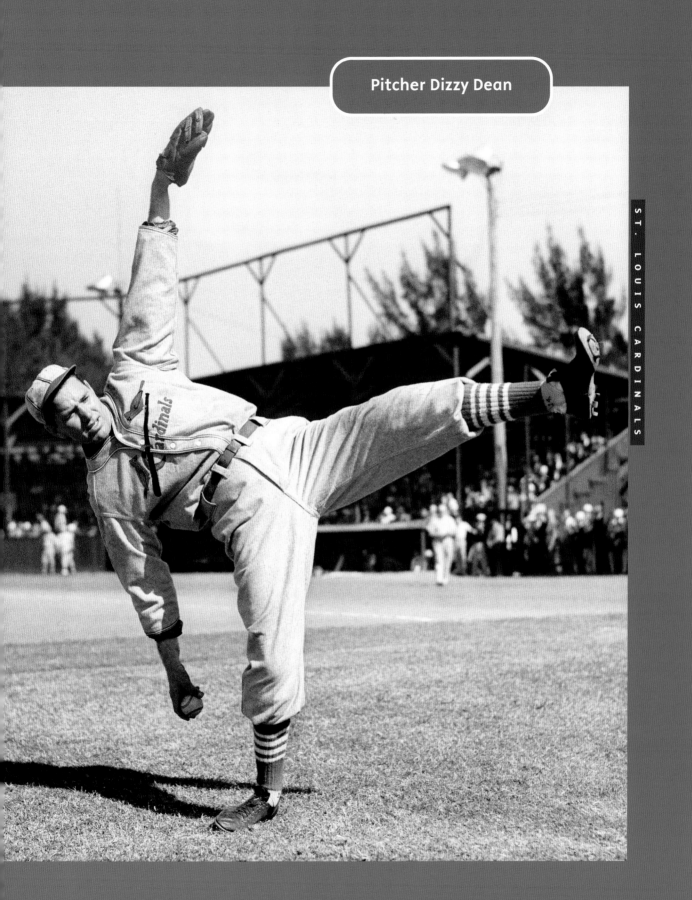

Pitcher Dizzy Dean

Outfielder Lou Brock

In the 1960s, speedy Lou Brock was a great hitter and base stealer. Pitcher Bob Gibson's fastball overpowered many batters. Brock and Gibson led the team to titles in 1964 and 1967. The Cards won the World Series again in 1982. Shortstop Ozzie Smith made many terrific fielding plays. Fans called him "The Wizard of Oz."

The Cardinals have made the **playoffs** 16 times since 2000. Catcher Yadier Molina helped them capture two more titles. He won nine Gold Gloves. The best fielders win them.

Other Cardinals Stars

Infielder Frankie Frisch played in four World Series with the Cardinals. He also managed the team to the 1934 championship. In 12 seasons with the Cardinals, first baseman Albert Pujols smacked 469 homers. His slugging helped him win three NL Most Valuable Player (MVP) Awards.

First baseman Albert Pujols

First baseman Paul Goldschmidt

t. Louis fans are counting on first baseman Paul Goldschmidt and third baseman Nolan Arenado. They hope those stars will bring another title to Busch Stadium soon!

About the Cardinals

Started playing: 1882

. . . .

League/division: National League,
  Central Division

. . . .

Team colors: red and navy blue

. . . .

Home stadium: Busch Stadium

. . . .

WORLD SERIES CHAMPIONSHIPS:

1926, 4 games to 3 over New York Yankees

1931, 4 games to 3 over Philadelphia Athletics

1934, 4 games to 3 over Detroit Tigers

1942, 4 games to 1 over New York Yankees

1944, 4 games to 2 over St. Louis Browns

1946, 4 games to 3 over Boston Red Sox

1964, 4 games to 3 over New York Yankees

1967, 4 games to 3 over Boston Red Sox

1982, 4 games to 3 over Milwaukee Brewers

2006, 4 games to 1 over Detroit Tigers

2011, 4 games to 3 over Texas Rangers

. . . .

St. Louis Cardinals website:
  www.mlb.com/cardinals

. . . .

Glossary

arch—a tall curved monument

....

playoffs—games that the best teams play after a regular season to see who the champion will be

....

rival—a team that plays extra hard against another team

....

stadium—a building with tiers of seats for spectators

....

title—another word for championship

....

First baseman Mark McGwire

Index